1st edition 2018

First published in 2018
by Dylan Townsend
Dublin, Ireland.

www.dylantownsend.com
All rights reserved

ISBN 978-0-9567027-5-3

UNION

_____

A Poetry Book by Dylan Townsend

Poems

DALKEY GARDEN

Flittering scarpal of wispy spider line holding
glint of eye.

Whispering with shimmeration, the glowmaker
shares its treasure in spittering swatches of show.

Dancing with the wind, each shuttle presenting
an angle of beauty so deep in rectified religion.

The great wusher sends more surprises with
tinkle tankles bouncing off the glory colours of
tree and hedge.

Robins attracted by stillnesses input, scarp about
searching for survival treasure, singing about
peace, love and the eternal truths the earth
efforvates.

Wufttling about, wiggling for the wind,
allofitandus, flouncing in the hynoptic ways of the
maker.

Inside dealt softness, outside touching peace, the
garden a symphony, an ovation of life, of pulse
and of grand brevity.

In the essence I sit; gone. An atom without charge
finding little resistance.

Perhaps I shall become a tree.

INDECISION A DECISION

You hum and haw your next direct, its tantalizing
and special, a place of undetect.

Its going to be amazing, once decision is made,
you will find the path and never
look(pastpresentornext)

But as decision becomes indecision, your best to
leave it all alone... for in that non-know there is a
decision bestown.

You may think its right to pontificate, right to
wander the course, it may be your undoing, to
push decision beyond endorse.

Sometimes there is nothing to do, simply smiling
at in-action, laughing at your un-do, potentially
more profitable then glambouring around on your
ninny-nuu.

Were all fumbling about, listening to decisions
that were not meant for us, the key is in the
listening, the waiting and the indecision,
evaporating with a clear and steady thought.

For its all so complicated, when we act after
wondering, the first decision is a clean mind
prohibiting the stumbling.

When standing, walking, running and screaming, keep on doing what your doing, your decision has already been made (or unmade)

MATTER Vs SPIRIT

Save me from this experience of true love she said. Of dreams fulfilled of futures gathered and seen. Its in the matter where we fled, she said. We are in the sky of eternal in spirit, he said.

The family will be kept comfortable in matter, she said. The family does not matter in the sky of dreams, he said. Every earthbound need is met, every trapping and cage on the ground is get.

The spirit plane is all we need, to share to love and forget our greeds. I will forget only our love and be saved from this life of higher purpose, she said (in unreality) A choice of death, a choice so oft we choose, the Gods of spirit know who really wins and those who choose the lose.

He said, she said. Actions; separated.

FINDING THE VOICE

Journey waltzed me Himilaya, up the steps and down the steps.

Chats, tales and solitary mountain thoughtdrifts.

You approach the pinnacle saluting your fear of non-triumph, scaling your worry of rocks and snowcap, falling otherside virginal.

Twinkling down the slope of victory, its in a state of glee that you are stopped, asked for vapor of herb and share in that togethered inhale.

The porter walks on, you syncing in with the rock, self and victory of self value.

Then begins the sound-chuwakasantikalumanuzunga... softly at first, with each step, blurts of sound finding their way into the ether of rocks and valley.

Chakalibulaatizattaramachukatiizambuksuganga coozillum! The valley pulses an echo, refracting the fruits of loneliness.

The wind joins company, wuffering dirt and rock, whirling around zone I a spell of wush!

Eckazummullajumunazygatronzyballjamdicozath izathyzathy!!

With the relish of pulsing bodily eruption, rustle stampedes at every cell of space, of timeless, godful zone everything.

Zwuthering into a crescendo of life totality.

This is it. The unison of everything.

Wind. All. Still.

The voice is found, the mind has arrived and it falls back below, waiting to be once again unbound.

LUCKY

There is a she to every he. Finding compliment can take it out of ya.

Salutations, made up connections and want be's rattle the cage of feelings pass, on path to luck.

The scenarios of 'this is it' are so multidutinous you catch doubt meddling in the thoroughfare of chapters that mujuddle could be and eternal.

Acceptance is nobodies friend, conforming or changing for that piece of heart; on the whim of betterance on the easyiest shortness, the most painful terminality.

The pouring search continues. Glimpses, glitters and kisses.

She was such a such, imagine.

Walking up stairs, falling down floors then sitting in your own chair, gripping the flanks "I love myself enough."

She wips round, black hair wraptapples that face, that one you knew was lucky.

You both throw it out there.

Future portending.

If there were superstitions for luck, they all

simultaneously combust, you depart but snickle the insides, knowledged that there will be a bump that escalates a volcano.

ZONE I

More of grab : less of have

More of give ; love will sieve

Hope forever and accomplishments will run reams.

Relationships are no work if your work is you.

Focus on love in all actions and all will prevail.

You will stand at the end of the day with wide open arms. The wind will take you away to within your cloud of content.

Besettled, behoned and Zone I.

THE HAPPINESS TOAD

Psychatropic totality is but one breathe away, the lung sweat of a toad meets the lungasm of ourselves. A song of sung in our ancient mind grasps the air and a man from the west bangs his thoracic of the sacred. We are brought through the net of ancient realities as gasp turns to agape as bridges of mythical fallow open to the eyestril of their.

We breathe through for love, we break through to forget shadow. The light of loves truth permeates all every, all every, all every.

Springing back into surrender of spinal bend of openevery, the cord of totality strings from the cosmos down to concinx, shooting waves of devastating beauty through the vessel.

(Body limp in orgasmic remembrance, ancient images flicker spectralic wonder into every cell)

We breathe through for love, we break through to forget shadow. The light of loves truth, permeates, permeates. Permeates.

The agape downloaded every cell, earthbound thoughts arrive asking for support. We hold eachother, the embrace of a thousand ages where we have sat for aoens anon. Here we pact, you run the stories through me and I will tell them in this vessel. She winks at me with a cheek of

know· scouring impossibility ·the burden laidened
and so to breathes action.

We go.

HOLISM

We are all here. Doing everything right now at the same time with the same body on a single globe.

Were almost complete but for our destructive un- one- nature that dominates.

We have the knowledge though.

Weareonesystem. Waiting for a unification of the parts which could bind a shared reality.

Building on goodness of humanity. Moulding with trust, love and thriving on our endeared stasis, whole is better then fragmented.

One big family, sharing inherent wisdom, getting along and moving forward on a shared line.

All it would take is a magic moment and BANG!

Holistic humanity.

YOGINI

Still.

Body soft.

Mind marshmallowing now.

Curves of perfection melting over sync.

Around and back as the sun knows.

Body/mind becoming friendly with romance
blossoming.

Effort befalling effortlessness with mind
forgetting.

Rythmn of Asana mounts podium of spiral.

Heartbeat asleep functioning unison.

Blood everywhere it is meant.

Movements become eureka's

Body integrity.

Still

(and then the real fun begins)

FLASHING SCENES

They glitter in thoughtbacks, trouncing into
memory with the glisten of new.

They are vivid with particulars, rough with
portend and all are not light.

There is fear, loathing and jealousy with love,
openness and adoration. The scenes are layered,
so much I trust them.

Conscious events come from unknown quarters,
its these flashing scenes uttering tones of happen.

Everything we need to know is there, blinking at
us in daily and in the scenes. Deciphering such
information is the mastery of modern life.

Choosing this and neglecting that, these are the
truths unveiled in those glaring flashing scenes.

One eye open and one closed.

HEALER OF THE HIDDEN

To sit with a man approaching end, cuddle disease on compassions utter, A man of demon turned to peace, from light to light who said his piece.

Ushered on destiny's tongue, she flickers dream into happen, appearing to share. Here my dear friend is cuddled by angel until last breathe offers cosmos.

A directory of tools unravel into space of between, ancient wisdoms converge modern truths into factality. The healer spells a web casting for higher purpose, we all are in love with these thoughts of perfect.

Perfect truths said perfectly in mantra repetition, the jewels apparate in spittering swatches of show, twisting know back and forth to the drumbeat of magic, mother earth feels these spells and smiles a million dimples.

She dots our lives like a wind of ferocity, swirling gifts to settle into and digest, she is gone now, her healing pulsing through us and this land et al.

THE CLAP

Making noise. Appreciative echo's overmuching a decibel awarding on the stage absorbing.

People gleam.

The heart pours an entertainment spew, crowds rejoice your creative spruce.

Efforts culmination

Louder and louder the clap escalates, sending energy to the bowing just made.

Filling up

Ovation signs the worth clause, audience giving thanks applause.

Gratitude epiphany

.....The curtain draws and both sides of the stage voke elation, reflecting a smile that will

domino

WHEN YOU DON'T KNOW WHAT TO WRITE BUT YOUR WRITING

Snap snap snap. Poetry shellshock. Needs an electrozode, not numb but squashy, stoned to staring with the will intact.

Like needing cigarette, pen wants his game, desires that lefty righty scroll of think. Blank.

Shoelaces yes there is a subject, a master of lexiconic volution an encyclopedia to follow.

As the speed at which day becomes night, the hand wakes mind wakes hand and flowasis has been reinstated so lets flock to the unknown... visit cosmic revelation, profound convention and get all there is to get. Blank.

HOLOTROPIC HUMANITY

From zygote mrathering backswatch to the cloudground, we fluff in unison, hale to in, ex to bliss... its here in breath that truths are exposed, where trixiebells, fairlyglads and the hyperbole of subconscious meet the clarity of a thousand moments combusted into one.

Its gajimbiliskibranbunskarandariiiazytheryzamguss atron as they say in the up!

The vortex's teaching infinity, the endless blue a place for all of us to inhabit. With focus and intent, all that we envision will be ours.

It's the unclouded in the internal zygote that's required, a place for us to heal, a place to shine, a zone of holotropic humanity.

Where we all reside.

CHAOS

The spontaneous evolution of nano-time is the grok to now!

Happening doing happening on

All angles are obtusity and brain springels jide and jupe to life's ebb.

Happening on happening doing.

Residing in the that, jive a celebrity of action, perching with up there... we all find ourselves in the ring of be.

Here now here zoom.

Focus bounces in the speed of interaction and smiles abound in the centre of what-this-go

Zoom-here-here-now!

It goes on around us. We are part, everything is all happening right here and at the beginning and end; it still will be chaos.

PERMUABLE

Jovial cracklesnap of spring tort; Christen me
Jerry and Pop Champagne to the nethertoast. Its
never burnt.

Porous Pumpkin shoots in the graveyard of
growth's commemoration ·there's a joker at hand·
punking the Freudian cracklewip of all
wondrance.

To the seedling core.

Thick skins wrestle down the tube to slink, drum
beating the clank for the audience of spring. April
was indifloquent on such the sychance and
participants chinned up at the show : glancing
down the eye of winters forgotten.

A swoop swappled.

Cuckoo went compass zrazy, swashing the
grooves into multii's. Tangles met of litigation
marred rainbows into bowties and the crash of
tweet blumbled the thunder of wooference.

Notwhatgotten does.

Chilli stuck tosh onto its backache, pulsating
properly, daffodils dwained and yes waived at
births egg and chicken. Spoons understanding
their destiny to utilise elipses.

Shadows photoshopped.

Laces tied brightly shook off the frost, tackling grey, asking palms of palette to paint purpose. Click spacker spluck and loop.

Formutation in continue.

UNISON

A noise utters in a momentum. Objects of animation are racing together, the air is silk that flutters by.

Sending signals with flap, each wurtling wander is a message to behold. On the eyes, in the heart.

That togethered frequency, that shared spirit is bound in fusion and trust of one-another.

It's the trust of the man coming up and the sun going down, it's the arriving without excuse and finding something beautifully elegant in the aspect of your doing.

Walking is one of the ultimate's. Simplistic, a fortress of trust, a place where equality is found.

There are lessons and then there is flying.

HOLDING THE UNREALISED

Grappling onto memories is easier then making new ones. All have a scorned past but not all are free of it to make an untainted future.

Forgetting is a denial while releasing is the souls way of smile. Unburdened we flounce lightened, absorbing the newxt's with plendent glad.

Once we have ungrappled, its tail will try and way your way again, this test is will. Signs of the new will replace the holded onto, unregistered and impulse discarded and rut snapped.

Trust is the basis of all everything. Trust your own devotions and inner will; We could all be malleable to one another, loving eachother so why attach to the other.

HIGHER PURPOSE

Evolve to transcend the ways of herd, to share love of do with those of new, co-create a vision of accelerated here, re-belong the cherished sacred collective.

Breathes of godly other sucked in with fever, bowel to chest and shushumna to third eye, barriers of ego burst through the skull, holdings grasped but purpose now's intent.

Surrender below the celestial caress, Earth's bounty of ground of test, open all cells as a lifetimes nan-o-flick.

Ideas of truths disseminate all every the new earth a place, visions have been connected now we must proceed to it.

The higher purpose for all to find.

FLUTTER

Lub a dub spring ajing flop flut all adrenolinsin.

Parting a waterfallent drizresiding pretruteously
along port/starboard rock the boat which way
next· time dispensing the western lame game
care boundaries, intention spoked with day next
wordsendology alacening the perimeter to field an
isosoles.

Intuition hijacks over analysis paralysis, thinks
becoming do's and uninhibited ignited new's.
Unchasted the becoming of a something steps to
its unexpecting propling, flouncering in the
masquerade of prepared, the butterfly merchant
bargains with scared.

But the then nothing would come from any if your
existence stagnated on the lect of inhibits
diswarding and who wants a heart that thuds in
dub when it can flutter in lucidriant gwyorphia.

THANKS N PRAISE

A chalice raised to those who have petted your pavement,

A surface is smoother when there's those who glide upon the roughened spickles.

Soon and fast will jolt friction if you don't bow to receive and thank in heed those who lampled your need.

He without appreciated wont have the chance to anymore, every atom will ruttle back with a charge, love in large, to keep in divines perfect tributary.

Squirzzling over indebt tabulation for vulnerabilities sign in clause, giving overmuch is no labour lost.

A thought of show, means more to many then you'll know. Write that care, press those thought buttons n make 2 people's days.

MANTRA

Shifting decibels of overwhat to who knows. The gods, the plants, the everyanything.

Ancient tongue reaching ancient answers, the basis is the form, the original all teaching seeds.

Cups of tea to the mind, warming unconscious possibilities and energies. Sounds glorifying next's.

Repetition – repetition‐ repeat

Solutions being tickles out of their stubborn caves. Sanskrit loudening into a storm of intention.

Up and up, to the best best version, words being used sacredly and then it all crashes with an adverse thought.

Repetition‐ repetition – repeat

ON MARRIAGE

Husband and wife to be atoned, Must spend some time alone, For the oak tree and the Cypress grow not in eachothers shade, Even the strings of a guitar are alone though they quiver with the same music.

As life bakes history into your quilt, The most beautiful patterns will be constructed with more than one fabric, We weave together as the self shares to a connect, Wearing eachother in as beautiful a way, As Denis & Brinda are together today.

IN THE FLUTTERS

Prepare for the heart dare, hopping barriers of
social cusp, emotion dealing with first sput.

Smile peels across the would happy face, not a
hint of social distaste, regurge in buzz haste and
its off to the flutters.

Everybody is invited to the party; excited,
palpitation, hope and lust are there to boot and
fear, mistrust and social ya ya's left in the
internal curtain.

The intersect is spend (more) iferus, eyes pop
and atmosphere electrics, mini stars pop the
around and zing helps 2 become 1.

Its love at first sight but we must check the eyes
with dialogue, of course the heart knows, its as
ancient as love.

HOLO

Flat on a bed of sheets in a room of humans in preperation for the something of happen, perplexing over the breathwork to announce itself.

We anticipate deep dots of emotion in the thoughtscape.

Glistening the air, is the apprehension of unknown.

Breathes of words guide action into thoughtlessness.

Hyperventilation initiates, faster and deeper, faster and deeper, lower and higher... the worm hole of holotropic winks its eye, body feeling weightless and chest palpabusting upwards and inwards until mirages with colours circle the inside lense.

The room outside has gone the sound of air whistling in and out of frothing mouths has ceased... lying their, body has lost the battle of importance, the spiralic vortex is on show, the ticket is free with directed breathe, the worlds are there, blinking at us from the other moment asking to be realized...

Music of momentous quality rifles the breathe into images of purple heavens, amoebic and ancient friends of DNA and cells... beauty is transmitted through tribal drum taps, litanies of the indigenous and a million chirps of yes!

Bliss is home in holotropic thoughtscope, the rabbit hole is magical... jump down with me and them and everything until you meet your own stars!

TOGETHERED QUANTUPLE

The race to lovebubble is a verdant splash on the heartstrings. We flux and flow in our eternity, gleaming in the moments of our forevered embrace.

The touches are more and more adore, cannot get enough after the delicate many. It is in the construct of soft huggle that ancient wisdom lets everybody know things are right, things are holy and we are at the centre of ourselves.

You plant compassion in the core soil and out pops love surfing the wave of know. There are places in this outer/inner that feel secure and imbued with peace, inside the mouth of pulse, there finds a warmth of forever.

There are fleetings of anger which tributise the passion, magma over the soft mantle of our bodies. Purity, that is all, a love sitting so deep, there are no words just is'is.

Thank you ...... for being in my life.

BROTHERS

Split on age of destinies languid jut, fear and competition opening void.

To love again, farther then an easy anger. Abuse held close, as mothers grasp.

Apart now collide, embracing frustration the only rapture colluded.

Shared journeys of created merit, spat out as visions crumble.

Escaping dis-ease. Uncomfort thwarted.

Now to seperate again and be free, a little less agony since the womb departed.

Anon to release, anon to be found. My brother. My brother. Its time to for another round.

INTEGRAL

Words uttered, actions delivered. Promised
spoken, reality folding straight line of dotted
signature.

Vertebrae aligned with the tissue of decisions.

Muscles strengthened with following through on
closing. The full stop of thought the sexiest action
without the hallow hall of faulter, opposing the
true tunneling of happen.

The sophisto thought manifesting instant, a grace
of befoldment mirrored back.

Here now.

Matched up and through line winking at birthday
now's.

FOLLOWING ENERGY

Choices ripple along the nowduct of invitation.

Observing poised for action, feeling and feeling until natural waves and vessel forward.

To act in truths tributary disuages the leak of business. Energy infused draining lifeforce untoward vibration of height.

The sectors of filtered states, followed inward on a bank of correct. The decisions, language of power, concealed by slave words.

Knowing faithly, followed is energy listened. Energy dancing, spiraling on the hearts step. Mind disobeyed to God of guts guru.

Once arriving we feel further, listen deeper until invitation clarity. As energy arrives, its there, in this heightened moment we strike claim to magic's offering. Clarity, poise, on track with our own field of magnificence.

The End! (or beginning)

www.ingramcontent.com/pod-product-compliance
Lightning Source LLC
Chambersburg PA
CBHW031617040426
42452CB00006B/573